get shout or miss out!

contents

celebs

16 5 Steps To Steal Vanessa's Style
59 10 Superstar Hotties!

real-life

14 "I've Got Permission To Sleep At School!"
56 "My Horoscope Came True!"
70 "My Boyfriend Died For A Dare!"

horoscopes

51 Horoscope Heaven!

fun

8 Embarrassing Moments!
20 Mad About Mocktails!
30 Boys — The Facts!
50 What Lads Love!
58 A Best Mate Always…
72 Embarrassing Moments!
78 Picture Perfect!
88 Laugh Out Loud Laws!

quizzes

13 What's Your Shopping Style?

22 Is Trouble Your Middle Name?

28 The BFF Test!

45 Is He A Mate Or A Date?

49 What's Your Colour Match?

57 What's Your Secret Obsession?

76 What's Your Perfect Party?

82 Friend Or Frenemy?

83 Are You Body Confident?

86 What's Your Nail Polish Personality?

87 Are You Aiming For The A-list?

your world

6 Who's Your Kind Of Crush?

10 Growing Up Around The World

23 Moving House? Here's How…

46 Dealing With Dyslexia

74 10 Tips To Make You A Great Mate!

80 5 Great First Dates!

84 The Ex Factor

fashion

31 A to Z Of Wardrobe Essentials

77 Faux Fur Fabulous!

beauty

26 Winter Skincare Sorted!

90 Party Perfect!

Printed and published by D.C. Thomson & Co., Ltd., 185 Fleet Street, London EC4A 2HS. © D.C. Thomson, 2010. Whilst every reasonable care will be taken neither D.C. Thomson & Co., Ltd., nor its agents accept liability for loss or damage to colour transparencies or any other material submitted to this publication. All products available at time of press.

who's your kind of crush?

Do you always go for the same type of lad? Well, here's what it means...

YOU 💛... a lad you've never spoken to!

This means that you...
- Love daydreaming about lads
- Can be a bit shy
- Aren't even sure if you want a boyf!

YOU 💛... the lad that everyone fancies!

This means that you...
- Tend to follow the crowd
- Want to fit in
- Might not be all that confident...

YOU 💛... your best boy mate!

This means that you...
- Love to a have a giggle
- Are mega close to your mates
- Rate personality over looks — every time!

YOU 💛... the bad lad!

This means that you...
- Are a bit of a rebel
- Are always looking for adventure
- Live in the moment

YOU 💛... the same boy as your bezzie!

This means that you...
- Are mega competitive
- Love gossiping about boys!
- Compare yourself to others

embarrassing moments!

Put a smile on your face with these cool cringes!

Illustration by Laura Watton.

"I was on a date with my crush and we were getting something to eat, when I suddenly had to nip to the loo. I hurried off to the toilets, but when I ran in, the floor had been flooded and I slipped and fell! I was totally soaked! It looked like I had fallen in a swimming pool — it was a total nightmare! I tried my best to dry myself off with the hand dryer but it was no use, and when I walked out of the toilets, everyone was just staring at me like I was crazy! Luckily, my crush saw the funny side and walked me home! Cringe!"

ELLE, CHELSEA

RED-FACED RATING:

RED-FACED RATINGS:

GET OVER IT!   SLIGHTLY SHAMEFUL!    COMPLETELY CRINGEY!

■ "I was in English class, and I was so bored because our substitute teacher wasn't very good, so my mate and I were sending notes to each other to pass the time. We were writing really cringey stuff and it was a great laugh until the teacher caught us. He made me read out the note to the class and it was all about who my crush was and how much I fancied him! The whole class started laughing at me, including my crush, and I still get teased about it now! So cringey!"

MAGGIE, ESSEX

RED-FACED RATING:

■ "I was desperate to get my hair trimmed at the ends but I didn't want to spend any money on it, so I decided to do it myself. I was snipping away so carefully, trying to cut off all of the split-ends, when a bird suddenly crashed into the bathroom window! I got such a shock because of the noise it made, that I had accidentally chopped a massive chunk of my hair off! I ended up going to the hairdresser to get a really short cut just to fix it and now my crush says that I'm a man! How embarrassing!"

SHANNON, HULL

RED-FACED RATING: 😊😊

■ "I was out for a walk with my dog, when I spotted my crush and his mates up ahead. I decided to walk over to them as cool as I could, to say 'Hi'… big mistake! When I got closer to them, one of his mates kicked a football across the road and my dog started chasing after it! She ran so fast after the ball that she was dragging me along and I tripped over my lace and fell flat in this minging puddle! I was muddy and soaked right through and all of the boys were laughing at me for ages! Cringe or what?!"

LEIGH-ANN, KIRKCALDY

RED-FACED RATING:

■ "I was standing in line with my friends in the school canteen and was waiting to pay for my food. My crush was sitting over by his mates and I could see him looking over at me. As I was walking over to my table, I was trying my best to look cool in front of him, when all of a sudden this rat scurried across the ground in front of me! I screamed and accidentally threw my food everywhere! The whole hall was laughing at me and I was covered in all my messy food! And to make things worse — it was a toy rat! Cringe!"

KYLIE, SHEFFIELD

RED-FACED RATING: 😊😊😊

■ "I was shopping in town with my friends and we were going up an escalator when I spotted my crush and his mates coming down the other side. He was smiling at me, and I was smiling back when suddenly my skirt got caught in the escalator stairs! My mates and I were all freaking out, trying to pull me free, but we couldn't, until 'RIPPP!' Half of my skirt ripped off! My crush and his mates came up to see what was going on and were laughing at me and my shredded skirt! Total embarrassment!"

JOSIE, WELLINGBOROUGH

RED-FACED RATING:

Growing Up Around The World

All the teens on the other side of the globe aren't too different from you, honest!

Japanese Girls

Japanese girlies are crazy about fashion, and they like their clothes seriously cute! Hello Kitty, anyone? They heard of it first! And did you know that Gwen Stefani's fragrance range, Harajuku Girls, is also a reference to the Harajuku street fashion in Tokyo, Japan?

Yup, every Sunday loadsa Tokyo teens get all dressed up in their kooky outfits and then hang out in the streets, hoping that they'll get papped by fashion mag photographers in the crowd. It's all about being an individual and expressing yourself — and boy, do they do that!

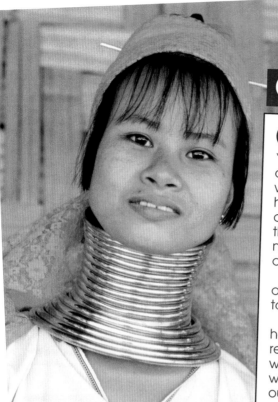

Giraffe Women

Girls from the Padaung tribe in Burma are known as 'Giraffe Women' due to the stack of brass rings they traditionally wear around their necks. They have their first rings fitted at around five… and by the time they're in their late teens their necks can have stretched to around 20cm long!

However, nowadays girls are able to choose whether they want to wear the rings or not — phew!

But get this… once your neck has been stretched, you can never remove the rings cos your head won't be supported! We think we'll stick to stacking bangles on our wrists, thanks!

USA Teen Queens

Loads of peeps are, like, totally potty about pageants in the USA! To be a teen beauty queen, you usually have to be between the ages of 11 and 19… and it's not just about standing there and looking pretty! Nope, you'll have to answer judges' questions, perform a talent and smile 24/7!

Beauty pageants aren't without their scandals, either — one teen queen was 'dethroned' after she ran out of a restaurant without paying the bill… leaving behind a bag that was rumoured to contain drugs! Uh-oh — that doesn't sound like appropriate beauty queen behaviour to us!

Jewish Girls

Jewish girls get thrown a special party called a Bat Mitzvah when they turn 12... lucky them! The party is to celebrate growing up, and the girl has to make a speech including the words, "Today I am a woman" — cringe alert! They can expect loadsa goodies, though — traditionally, cash is given in multiples of 18!

South African Girls

In the South African Ndebele tribe, a girl isn't allowed to see or speak to any lads (and that means ALL lads!) for three months after she starts her periods. We don't know what we'd do without our daily crush dose — especially seeing as the poor girlies have to stay inside learning ceremonial beadwork instead!
Er, fun.

what's your shopping style?

How do you spend those precious pennies?

start

Do you love spending ages going round the shops?

no → **You stick to wearing the same colours a lot.**

yes → **You go shopping at least once a week!**

You happily buy stuff from charity shops!

yes → **You only buy stuff you totally love!**

no →

yes → **You ♥ Alexa Chung's style!**

You can be mega lazy!

no →

yes →

You swap clothes with your BFF sometimes!

yes →

no →

You like your style to stand out!

You love buying stuff you see in shout!

yes →

no →

no

yes

Strictly High Street!

You know what you like and you stick to it! You have favourite shops which you visit, like, all the time and you always check out shout for the latest looks!

Internet Crazy!

You hate trawling round the shops and would much rather click-and-buy from the comfort of your own home! It's way easier and more fun!

Vintage, Darling!

You have a unique sense of style which makes you stand out! You prefer buying one-of-a-kind clothes than something everyone else has got, too!

13

"I'VE GOT PERMISSION TO SLEEP AT SCHOOL!"

Sarah keeps falling asleep in the strangest of places...

It happened for the first time about six months ago at school. I was sitting in my Maths class when I suddenly felt really sleepy. I felt like I'd not had any sleep the night before, when in fact I'd had an early night and at least eight hours in bed!

"I struggled to stop myself from just putting my head down on my desk but, before I knew it, I was soon fast asleep! It was only when my friend Demi shook me that I woke to find my teacher standing over me with a furious expression on his face!

"The whole class was laughing and my teacher went mad at me in front of everyone, which was *sooo* embarrassing! He accused me of staying up too late the night before and warned me that he'd get in touch with my parents if it happened again.

"My mates, of course, found the whole thing hilarious and joked that it was only a matter of time before someone fell asleep in class because Maths was so boring! I didn't understand why I suddenly felt the need to sleep, though — I wasn't even tired before it happened!

> **"The teacher accused me of staying up late."**

"I told myself that it was probably a one-off and I soon forgot about it until it happened again a few weeks later. I was eating lunch with some of my mates and a few hot lads in the canteen when I had to have a five minute nap — I literally just moved my lunch to one side and went to sleep! Everyone had a laugh about it when I woke up, but I was secretly worried…

"Mum made a doctor's appointment for me and he asked me heaps of questions about my sleeping habits, how much homework I had and how long I was spending watching TV and using my laptop. I was a bit disappointed when all he

ended up telling me was that tiredness is a teenage common problem and I should just try to get as much sleep as possible.

"Things slowly became worse over the next couple of months. I was falling asleep a couple of times a day and my teachers were starting to get pretty annoyed — and, when I fell asleep in Maths again, my teacher phoned my dad. Mum decided that enough was enough and that she was going to take me back to our doctor's surgery.

"We saw a different doctor and she referred me to a specialist at the hospital who said that he was almost certain I had a condition called narcolepsy, where the part of the brain that controls sleeping and waking doesn't work properly. He said that people with narcolepsy suffer from 'sleep attacks', where they feel an overwhelming urge to sleep — even in the strangest places!

"I was happy that someone finally believed there was something wrong with me, but a little upset when the doctor said there wasn't a cure for my condition yet. I was told to try to get up and go to bed at the same time every day and to do as much exercise as I could. My doctor also contacted my school and said I should be allowed to take 'sleep breaks' whenever I needed to — without getting into trouble!

"Making the suggested changes has really improved my narcolepsy. I still fall asleep sometimes, though — one really embarrassing time was when I was out for a meal with one of my mates and her posh relatives! Narcolepsy makes my life more difficult in some ways but I'm used to it now, and so are my mates. I just hope that there will be a cure for it one day!"

> **"I'm allowed to take 'sleep breaks' when I need to."**

{ Make like Zac's girl and look fabulous! }

5 steps to steal Vanessa's style!

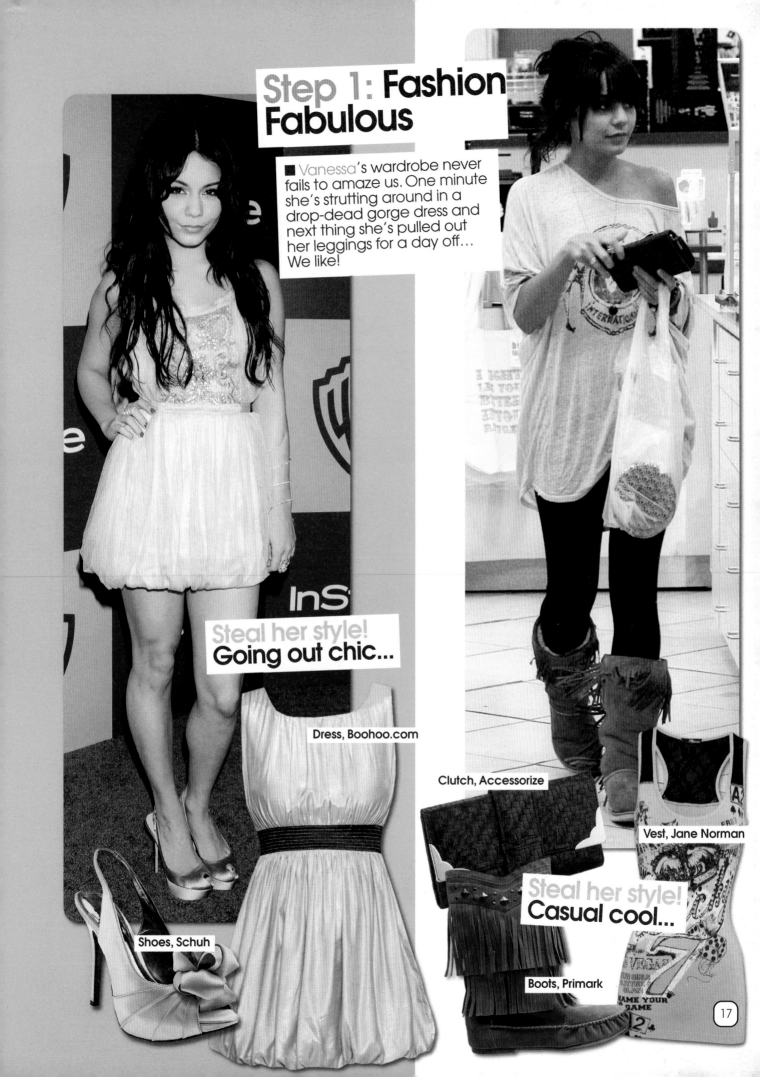

Step 1: Fashion Fabulous

■ Vanessa's wardrobe never fails to amaze us. One minute she's strutting around in a drop-dead gorge dress and next thing she's pulled out her leggings for a day off… We like!

Steal her style!
Going out chic...

Dress, Boohoo.com

Shoes, Schuh

Clutch, Accessorize

Vest, Jane Norman

Steal her style!
Casual cool...

Boots, Primark

17

Jewel genius...

Ring, Freedom
at Topshop

Cuff, Accessorize

Step 2: Amazing Accessories

■ A cool bangle here, some beads there, and rings galore — *Vanessa*'s never short of an accessory or two…

Necklace, George at Asda

Glam denim...

Clutch bag,
Internacionale

Shoe boots,
George at Asda

Belt, New Look

Step 3: Red Carpet Make-up

■ Smoky eyes are standard protocol for the red carpet and V shows hers off to perfection.

Steal her style!

▥ Start with shadow and build up a dark charcoal shade from the middle of your lids out towards the outer corners. Blend in a slightly lighter, metallic shade on the rest of the lid. Apply a little highlighter on the brow bone to make sure there are no harsh lines.

▥ Heaps of mascara will ensure your lashes don't go unnoticed…

▥ Finish with the must-have — black kohl pencil, neatly smudged under lower lashes. You can always try dark brown for a softer look!

Step 4: Glowing Skin

■ What we wouldn't do for that radiant skin which always seems flawlessly healthy and gleaming… But, trust us, it *is* possible!

Steal her style!

▥ Get plenty of sleep — you don't see Vanessa pulling an all-nighter like la Lohan, do you?!

▥ Find a great fake tan — a natural shade applied to your face once or twice a week will keep you from feeling pale 'n' pasty.

▥ Highlighter and shimmer creams are your new best friends. Apply before bronzer for a natural, sophisticated look.

Step 5: Superstar Hair

■ Vanessa's trademark locks are rarely seen looking dull… Gorgeous waves make sure they're always shiny.

Steal her style!

▥ Treat your tresses to a once-a-week pamper sesh with a deep conditioner.

▥ If you've got naturally curly hair, scrunch salt water through damp hair and leave to dry naturally for V's look.

▥ If you've got straight hair, apply a volumising mousse after washing, then use giant tongs when dry.

19

mad about

Mocktails are *the* hottest party drink this winter — they look really cool and taste sooo good! Here's some great recipes to try out!...

The Essentials
As well as your fave drinks, you'll to need this little lot:
- Cocktail shaker.
- Fruit.
- Grenadine syrup.
- Umbrellas, straws, etc.
- Ice.

Crazy Christmas Cranberry Crush
● This one's our fave and it's *sooo* easy to make! You'll need cranberry juice, orange juice, cola, a splash of grenadine and some honey to add the finishing touches. All you've got to do is mix the ingredients in a cocktail shaker, pour into a fancy glass and add some ice. Mmmm!

Cinderella: Lemon juice, orange juice, pineapple juice, grenadine and ginger ale.

Hurricane: Orange juice, cranberry juice, grapefruit juice, apple juice and a slice of orange.

Boston Cooler: Ginger ale and vanilla ice-cream!

mocktails!

Learn how to make stunning party drinks!...

Pineapple Passion

● Just mix pineapple juice, passion fruit juice, one tsp of lemon and one tsp of grenadine — add some ice, stir well and get ready to be refreshed! Treat your tastebuds!

Apple Pie Mocktail

● You'll need some apple juice, one tsp of lemon juice, half a tsp of grenadine syrup, crushed ice and a slice of orange. *Sooo* indulgent!

Green Alien: Lemonade, lime juice and a slice of lime.

Shirley Temple: Ginger ale, orange juice and grenadine.

Crazy Cow: Apple juice, milk, and a slice of apple.

Dolce & Gabanna: Diet cola and grenadine — DC & G!

Berry Patch: A handful of blueberries, strawberries and raspberries with vanilla ice-cream and milk.

Orangatan: Orange juice, cranberry juice and a slice of orange.

IS TROUBLE YOUR MIDDLE NAME?

Find out if you're good, or a good girl gone bad!

START

You've never had a detention — y / n

Your school reports are always great! — n

Your friends' ❤ parents you! — n

You always speak your mind — y / n

You never answer back — n / y

You're, like, totally late for everything! — y / n

Ke$ha's your idol! — n / y

You never argue with your 'rents! — n / y

You're always falling out with your mates! — y / n

It's true — you've got a real mean streak! — n / y

You're a good girl!
You're kind-hearted and patient — and always do what you think is right. Remember to let your hair down and say what you think sometimes, though!

You're sometimes a sinner!
Sometimes you're nice as pie, and sometimes you're a total diva! You've pretty much got the balance right, but try to show your good side more than your bad!

You're totally troublesome!
Well, well, well, missy! You can be pretty rude and mean sometimes — but there's a nice girl in there somewhere! Just think how your behaviour affects others before you act, and you'll be nicer in no time!

Moving House?
Here's How...

Boxed-up belongings and mates that are miles away… could it get any worse?
Here's how to stop your move from turning into a total 'mare…

New You!

■ You can be whoever you want to be! Stuck with a cringey nickname cos you did something shameful, like, a million years ago? Got a rep for being super sensible just cos you've never kissed a boy before — like, big whoop, btw! Moving house is a great way of saying bye-bye to bothersome baggage. No longer will you have to answer to the call of Smelly Ellie, which can only be a good thing!

■ Keep in touch! Facebook is a great way of keeping yourself in the loop, and let's be honest, you probably spent more time messaging your mates on the old FB than speaking to 'em in 'real life', anyway! OK, so you might not get to see them as often, but all those stand-in-front-of-the-class-and-introduce-yourself cringes are never as bad when you've got a bunch of mates to share it with!

Please Yourself!

■ OK, you officially have no friends, at least none who are close enough to save you from dying of boredom over the weekend. However, now you've got the chance to do exactly what YOU want to do… If you've spent every Saturday in distant memory trailing around the shops after your mates when you'd much rather have been tucked up with *The Hills* boxset then, guess what? You can!

Hello, Boys!

■ Look at it positively! Like, should we mention that *Twilight*'s Bella Swan moved away and bagged the love god himself, Edward Cullen? Surely you don't need a better example than that?! If you're still mourning that fact that you'll never see your crush again (even though he hadn't said two words to you in as many years!) then you're missing out. Time to check out the local talent, missy!

Making Mates!

■ Obviously, you're going to be on the hunt for some new friends. The best way to sniff out some peeps that you have something in common with is by joining clubs — that way it's easy as pie to get chatting! For the rest of the time, just be smiley and approachable — and don't stress! You *will* make new mates, even if you do think you're destined to be loner for the rest of your life!

winter skincare sorted!

Everything you need to know about glowing for it this winter!

Yep, our skin changes throughout the year and can be affected by lots of things — sun, wind, central heating and even stress at school can make a difference to the way your skin looks and feels...

If your skin's OILY like Miley's...

❏ You feel like your skin doesn't need moisturiser (but actually it does!).

❏ Your face, especially your t-zone (forehead, nose, chin) becomes shiny throughout the day.

❏ Sometimes your skin breaks out and you're prone to the odd blackhead or two. Grrr...

You'll ♥... Dermalogica Clean Start Welcome Matte SPF15 Moisturiser.

If your skin's DRY like Alexa's...

❏ After washing, your skin can feel tight and uncomfortable — moisturiser is a must!

❏ Your skin never looks shiny and you sometimes feel like you need to reapply moisturiser during the day.

❏ The occasional red or even flaky patch can pop up — what a pain!

Must-have... E45 Endless Moisture Replenishing Care Cream for Dry to Very Dry Skin.

If your skin's NORMAL like Vanessa's...

❏ You hardly ever suffer from spots, even if you don't bother about looking after your skin — tut tut!

❏ Although at times your skin can become dry or oily, it always gets back to normal, no problem — lucky you!

❏ Your complexion doesn't tend to react to using new products, sensitive skin isn't an issue.

Face washing fun... Neutrogena Wave.

How Your Skin Can Look This Hot...
All Winter Long!

Just looking at Lauren's cool complexion is enough to have us running to the beauty counters in Boots, filling our baskets with fake tan and face masks... But before you splash the cash, check out these top tips to make sure winter skin probs don't spoil your party season!...

"I always wear bronzer because I love the way my skin looks when it's tan!"

NO *Dry Lips*

We're guessing Jennifer Aniston has the softest pout in Celebville after hearing that she regularly uses a little sugar and warm water on a toothbrush to lightly scrub her lips. Along with your D.I.Y. lip scrub, avoid licking your lips and keep a balm to hand at all times (this'll work a treat on red noses, too!).

NO *Red Faces*

Stepping out the door and being greeted by a force ten gale each morning isn't exactly great fun for your face! So put a stop to red, upset skin with these no-brainer skin savers...

DON'T wash your face (or hands) in really hot water — higher temperatures actually dry out your skin.

DO use a moisturising face mask at least once a week, and a rich moisturiser every day (all over!) to help your skin's natural barrier against the elements!

NO *Damaged Skin*

Yes, it's winter. And, yes, the sun does seem to be a distant memory from months ago... but, no, that doesn't mean we can forget about SPF (sigh)... Selena Gomez says she works it into her beauty regime! "I use a light coat of Oil Of Olay SPF lotion and let it dry a little bit before I put my make-up on."

NO *Flaky Fake Tan*

Winter weather can dry out even the most moisturised skin, making fake tan application more of a minefield than ever before!

Beat the flake by keeping bronzed with a daily tanning moisturiser and for those all-important Christmas parties, body scrubs are your new BFF.

Kim Kardashian reveals she "uses a body scrub all over" before getting her salon spray tan. Follow up with an oil-free moisturiser when you step out of the shower, then make sure you're completely dry before applying tanning lotion. Simples!

27

the BFF test!

Great mate or mate hate? Find out below…

What to do —
Just tick the box that's right for you!

1 Your mate wants you to come watch her boyf play for the school footie team but you think sports are so boring! You…

▮ Tell her 'No'! Well, her boyf's team will probably get beaten anyway!

▮ Go and stand in the pouring rain, in silence, listening to her bang on about how great he is!

▮ Go and have fun checking out all the other buff boys!

2 You hear that your bezzie has been starting some rumours about you behind your back! You…

▮ Start a life-wrecking rumour about her and laugh as she suffers through it!

▮ Tell everyone it's true, because you don't want to call her a liar…

▮ Talk to her about it and try to sort it out calmly!

3 The hottest party of the year is this weekend and your mate wants to borrow the coolest outfit in your wardrobe! You say…
- Yeah, right… As if!
- Well, I was going to wear it, but it'll probably look better on you…
- Cool, but could I borrow your necklace to complete my killer outfit?

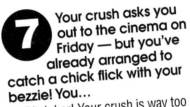

4 You ask out her crush for her, but he says he would rather eat his own underpants than go on a date with her! You tell her…
- Everything he said, but with some painful add-ons, just for a laugh!
- That he's thinking about it, and that it's looking good!
- That she's way above his league!

5 Your mate has just turned up with the worst haircut ever! You…
- Burst out laughing, then ask if she cut it herself… with a lawnmower!
- Tell her that you love it *sooo* much!
- Hint that maybe the new 'do doesn't suit her as much as the last one.

7 Your crush asks you out to the cinema on Friday — but you've already arranged to catch a chick flick with your bezzie! You…
- Ditch her! Your crush is way too hot to turn down!
- Tell him 'No', because you want to keep her happy…
- Arrange a big group trip to the cinema and keep everyone happy!

6 You've just found out that you and your BFF have the same crush! You…
- Get in there before she does!
- Decide to fancy someone else, even though you don't really want to…
- Have a laugh with her, chatting about how hot that guy is!

8 Your friend has asked to copy your homework AGAIN, but you know she wouldn't let you do the same! You…
- Give her all of the wrong answers — that'll show her!
- Give in to her and be secretly annoyed!
- Suggest that you two should do your homework together in future.

Mostly Pink…
Wow! We're shocked that you actually have any mates! You always think of yourself first and for some freaky reason, you kinda enjoy dissing your bezzie and laughing at her problems… How mean are you?!

Mostly Green…
You're a bit of a wimp, really! You let your mates take advantage of your good nature and you totally need to stick up for yourself more. Let your bezzie know that she should treat you as well as you treat her!

Mostly Blue…
It's official — you're a great mate! Keeping a good friendship is a high priority to you and you know that it's all about give and take. Plus, you're, like, the best at helping out your mates when they need it the most! We wish we were your bezzie!

BOYS

JUST WHEN YOU THOUGHT THEY COULDN'T GET ANY WEIRDER!...

— THE FACTS!

68% of teen lads sneak a look at the problem pages in girls' mags!

11% said they'd go on a date with a girl they didn't fancy cos they think it makes them look more attractive to other girls!

Kissing on the first date? Yes please, say 59% of boys!

A shameful 94% said they'd rather watch footie than go on a hot date!

77% of teen lads think girls are crazy!

Awww — 62% said they've got no idea how to ask a girl out!

41% think it's OK to use mouthwash instead of brushing their teeth — talk about lazy!

A shocking 23% said they'd dump a girl if she put on weight!

51% think looks are more important than personality!

97% said they get embarrassed by PDAs in front of their mates — you have been warned, girls!

A to Z of wardrobe essentials

shout's rundown of the clothes every fashionista should own!

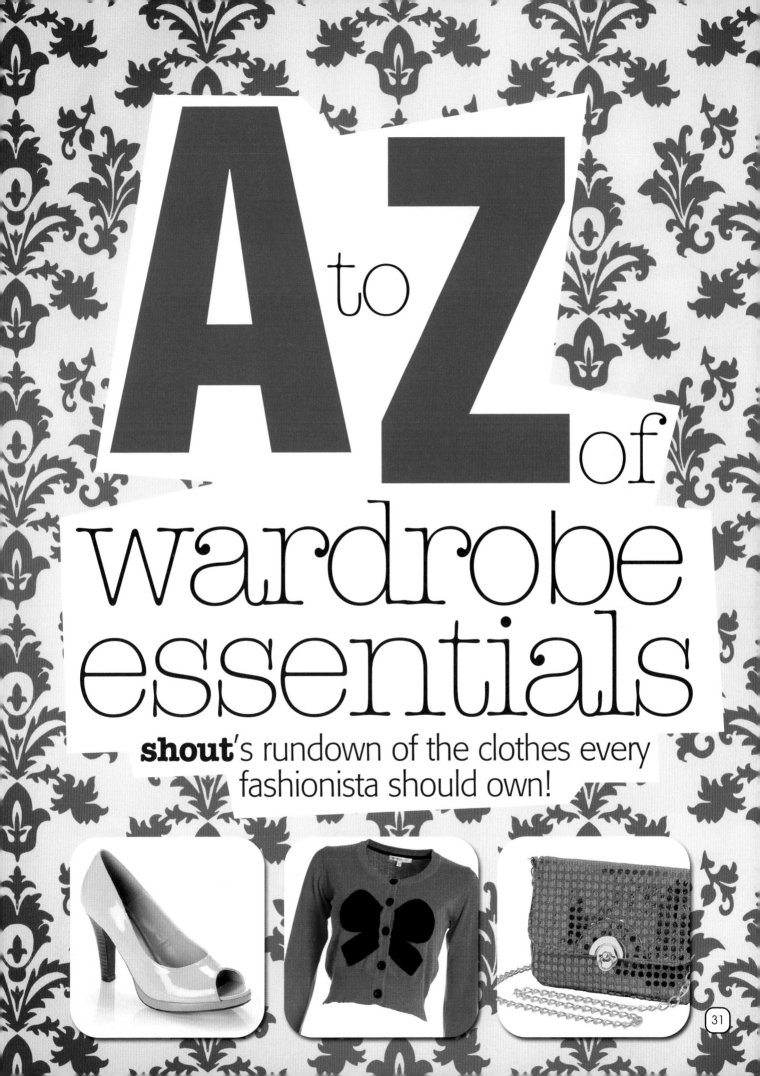

a Amazing Heels!

★ Sooo much fancier than a pair of ballet flats! Heels will give you height, elongate your legs — and not to mention make you feel a million dollars!

Barratts

Jane Norman

Tammy at BHS

VV Brown!

Matalan

Accessorize

Internacionale

A-wear

B Big Bag!

★ Carry all your day-to-day essentials in a beautiful big bag! Pick a colour that matches most of your wardrobe and experiment with styles like quilted, patent or studded!

Accessorize

32

Primark

Internacionale

Primark

C Chanel Chic!

★ **Every fashionista loves Chanel — and we can see why!** Coco Chanel's designs were all about monochrome simplicity which every girl can carry off. Try the look yourself!

Ring, Internacionale

Bangles, Primark

River Island

D Denim

★ **Uh, duh! Of course denim was going to appear in our A-Z! Jeans are the staple piece of millions of wardrobes all over the world. Here are a few of our faves…**

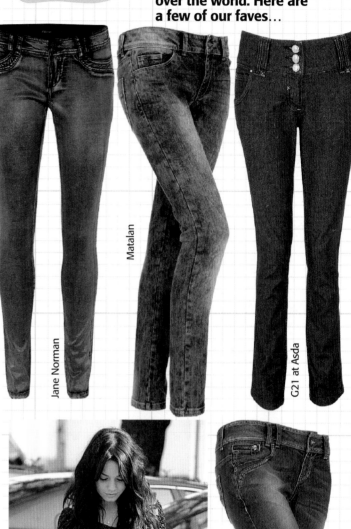

Jane Norman

Matalan

G21 at Asda

Jane Norman

Vanessa Hudgens!

e Easy-to-wear Dresses!

★ Sometimes, jeans and a T-shirt just doesn't cut the style mustard for everyday chic, and we reckon that a cute day dress is a great alternative! Try leggings, a cardigan, and flat shoes to complete the look!

New Look

People Tree

River Island

Lindsay Lohan!

George at Asda

Girls Limited at M&S

Primark

f Feel Cosy!

★ Day-time = chunky knit
Evening = fine knit

G21 at Asda

Miss Selfridge

ASOS.com

Tammy at BHS

Accessorize

Evie at Peacocks

Tammy at BHS

Great Leg-spectations!

★ **Don't be a slave to dull tights — spruce things up with colours or patterns!**

Head-turning Accessories!

★ **Add some va-va-voom to your look with the help of a bold hairband! You're gonna want big locks for this look, so tip your head upside down, spray hairspray into roots, flip your head up — and muss it up!**

Boohoo.com

Andrew Barton at Tesco

Dorothy Perkins

Kelly Osbourne!

Schuh

George at Asda

Tu at Sainsbury's

Matalan

Jane Norman

i In Step!

★ For day-time chic, invest in a pretty pair of pumps! They're mega versatile, too — wear 'em with jeans, skirts and dresses!

Boohoo.com

New Look

Primark

Matalan

J Jackets!

★ We totally can't live without our cosy winter coat… Well, unless we move to a hot country!! Invest in a quality jacket and you're sorted all winter!

Gossip Girl's Jessica Szhor!

Primark

Evie at Peacocks

Boohoo.com

Killer Curves!

★ Ooh, waist belts! You've gotta love 'em for accentuating your shape!

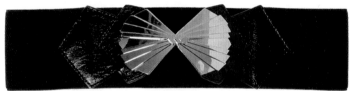
Jane Norman

Primark

Evie at Peacocks

Pixie Lott!

Lush Legs!

★ Our summer saviours! All hail the wonders of leggings!

New Look

New Look

New Look

Next

Idol at New Look

Fearne Cotton at Very.co.uk

37

m Ma-hoo-sive Jewels!
★ **Instantly change a look with jumbo jewels!**

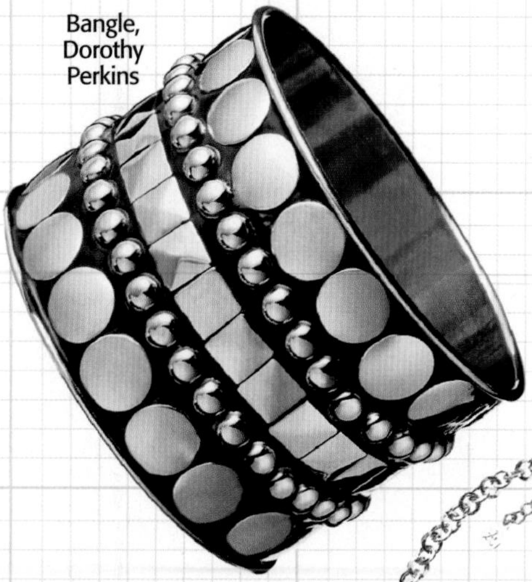

Bangle,
Dorothy
Perkins

Ring, Freedom
at Topshop

Bangle,
Primark

Necklace, Accessorize

Necklace, Freedom
at Topshop

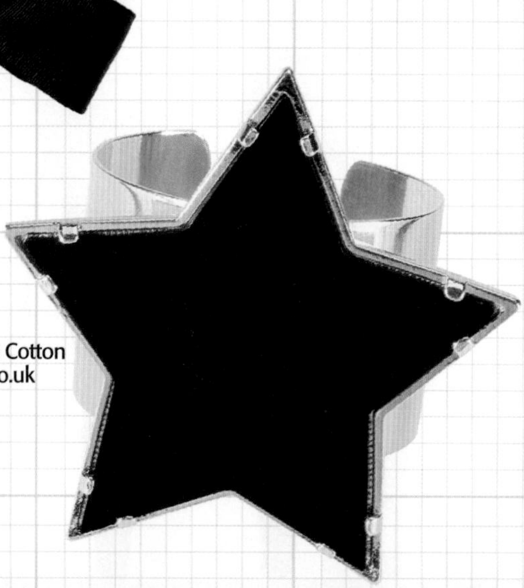

Cuff, Fearne Cotton
at Very.co.uk

n Nice 'N' White!
★ **Get more use out of your school shirt by pairing it with jeans or cool high-waisted shorts, just like Nicole Richie!**

Paul's Boutique at Bank

Nike

New Look

O Ooh, Comfy!

★ Mmmm, hoodies are the best fashion fix for lazy days. Pair 'em with jeans or shorts and keep cosy!

Sienna Miller!

P Plain T-shirt!

★ Yep, stock up on these, girls! They're the ultimate wardrobe staple! You can update your look with jewellery, scarfs and cardigans or wear them under dresses for a more casual approach.

Matalan

Bay

Internacionale

Bag, Accessorize

Love Bug

Matalan

Purse, Primark

Q Quids In!

★ You can get a lot of cute buys that'll spruce up your wardrobe from only £1 (Primark, anyone?)! Go shopping once a month for these little treats!

Badges, RocknRose

Hair clips, Tammy at BHS

r Riding High!

★ **Pretty ladies — get your high waisted skirt here! We love the look paired with a casual T-shirt… Lush!**

Primark

A-wear

Be Beau at Matalan

Katie Price!

Sparkles & Shine!

★ Any diva will tell you that it's all about the sparkles! Grab attention with a gorgeous piece of arm candy — we love sequins in silver and pink. Mmmm!

Jane Norman

Accessorize

New Look

Matalan

Next

Time-less Classic!

★ Being on time is, like, *sooo* on-trend right now! Well, it is if you've got a gorgeous watch like this!

Oasis

u Underwear!

★ **Back to basics, fashionistas! Good fitting underwear will make your outfit sit better and make you feel great!**

Next

Red Herring at Debenhams

Tu at Sainsbury's

V Vest Top!

★ It's a summer staple, but don't banish them to the back of your wardrobe during the winter months — they're totally handy for wearing under jumpers, cardigans and dresses! The layered look always works!

Jane Norman

F&F at Tesco

H&M

Tammy at BHS

Tu at Sainsbury's

Rocket Dog
at Schuh

F&F at
Tesco

W Winter Boots!

★ Don't even think of stepping out in winter without a pair of boots on! Pumps are a seasonal no-no!

Internacionale

Faith

Linzi
Shoes

Schuh

X X-clusive Statement Dress!

★ Turn heads in an absolutely stunning dress! Go crazy with colour and sequins and wow your crush... we love red, pink, electric blue and emerald green!

Tammy at
BHS

Boohoo.com

Rise

Katy Perry!

y Yummy Gym Bunny!

★ **You look hot the rest of the time, so why should P.E. be any different?!**

New Look

Puma at Debenhams

New Look

Nike at Schuh

Peacocks

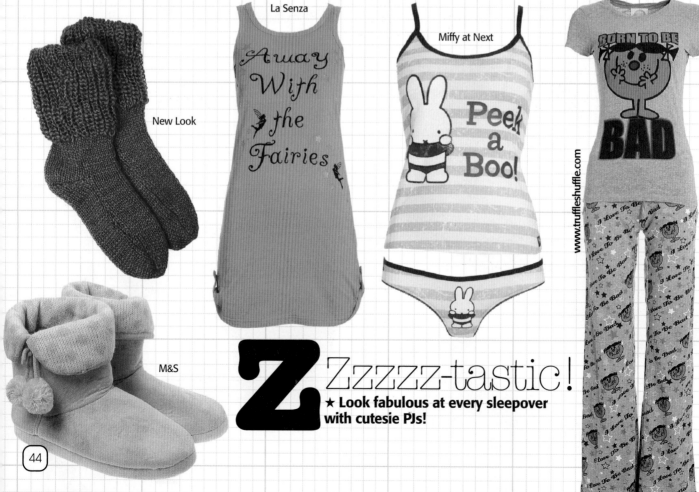

La Senza

New Look

Miffy at Next

Away With the Fairies

Peek a Boo!

BORN TO BE BAD

www.truffleshuffle.com

M&S

Z Zzzzz-tastic!

★ **Look fabulous at every sleepover with cutesie PJs!**

44

All products available at time of press.

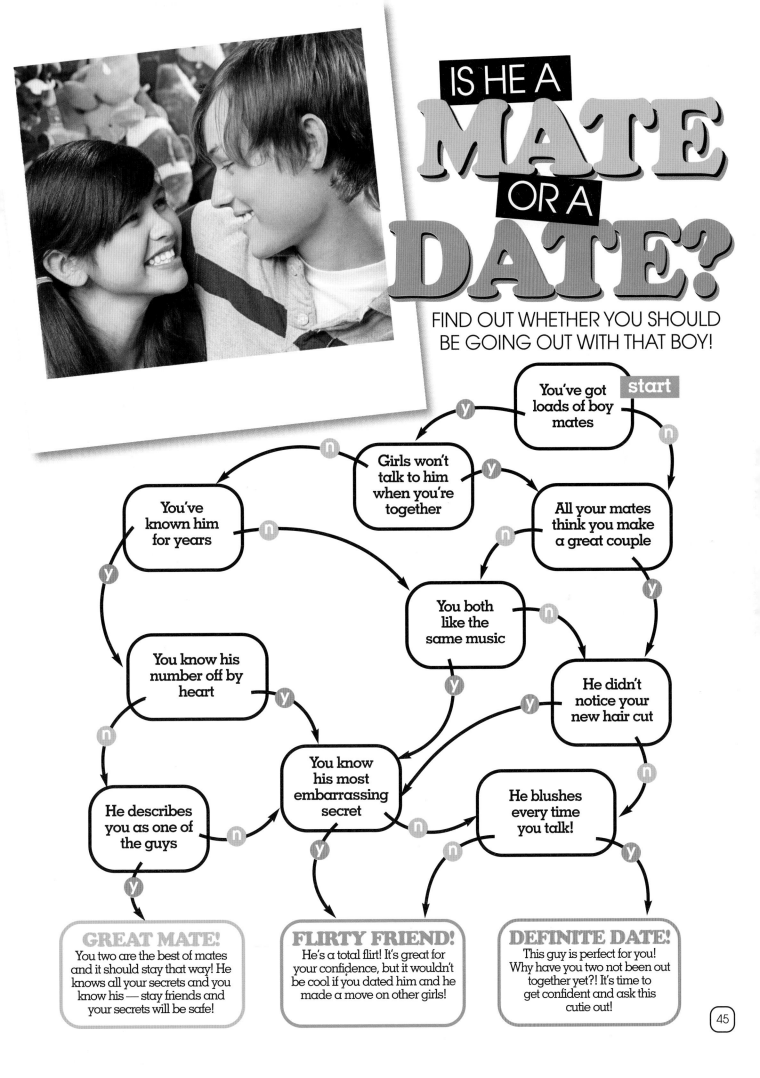

IS HE A MATE OR A DATE?

FIND OUT WHETHER YOU SHOULD BE GOING OUT WITH THAT BOY!

start

You've got loads of boy mates

Girls won't talk to him when you're together

You've known him for years

All your mates think you make a great couple

You both like the same music

You know his number off by heart

He didn't notice your new hair cut

You know his most embarrassing secret

He describes you as one of the guys

He blushes every time you talk!

GREAT MATE!
You two are the best of mates and it should stay that way! He knows all your secrets and you know his — stay friends and your secrets will be safe!

FLIRTY FRIEND!
He's a total flirt! It's great for your confidence, but it wouldn't be cool if you dated him and he made a move on other girls!

DEFINITE DATE!
This guy is perfect for you! Why have you two not been out together yet?! It's time to get confident and ask this cutie out!

45

Dealing With Dyslexia

Ever get nervous when you're reading out loud in class? Then try doing it with dyslexia…

WHAT IS DYSLEXIA?

Dyslexia is a learning disorder that affects the way you take in information, and it means that you might have difficulty with reading and writing. For example, you might find yourself mixing up pretty similar words like "won" and "now". It can affect people of ALL levels of intelligence and even really smart peeps can have dyslexia! Like, hello? Actual genius, Albert Einstein, anyone?

FACT

ABOUT **10%** OF THE UK POPULATION IS DYSLEXIC!

FACT

YOU CAN BE DYSLEXIC IN **ANY** LANGUAGE!

DO I HAVE IT?

In most cases, sufferers don't even know that they're suffering from dyslexia — in fact, they often think they're a lil' bit stupid! This is totally not the case at all, though! If you make continual errors with spelling, and feel sick every time you're asked to read out loud in class cos you know you'll struggle to sound out words correctly, then you might just have it…

SYMPTOMS INCLUDE…

- Being able to read a word on one page but not recognising it on another…
- Missing letters out in words, for example, reading "star" instead of "stair"…
- Feeling abnormally tired after reading a small passage of words…
- Mixing up similar-looking letters, such as q and p, and d and b…

A NON-DYSLEXIC PERSON WOULD SEE…

shout

BUT SOMEONE SUFFERING FROM DYSLEXIA MIGHT SEE…

sohut

FACT

DYSLEXIA TENDS TO RUN IN FAMILIES!

Celebs with Dyslexia

■ The Saturdays' Mollie King has never let dyslexia hold her back — she aced her exams at school!

■ Holly Willoughby revealed that she was dyslexic after some twits criticised her spelling on Twitter!

■ Orlando Bloom says, "Dyslexia is not due to a lack of intelligence, it's a lack of access." Thumbs up to him!

Kim didn't realise that she was suffering from dyslexia...

*Pic posed by model.

I'd never been smart at school. For as long as I could remember I'd been in all the bottom groups and I'd just kind of come to the conclusion that school wasn't for me. It's not that I was lazy or that I didn't try — I just didn't seem to pick things up as fast as other people!

"It really annoyed me, though… sometimes the teachers shouted at me when I made really basic spelling errors time and time again. I got really frustrated with myself as well — the mistakes I made were so silly, but I just couldn't seem to do anything about it!

"I always cringed whenever we had a spelling test because I always got pretty much the lowest score in the class — it was so embarrassing! All my friends were really brainy and seemed to do really well at school without even trying… I just wished it wasn't so hard for me.

"The one part of English I did love, though, was creative writing. I always had loads of ideas in my head but I just couldn't seem to get them onto paper the way I wanted. I never got good grades — even though the teacher always commented on my great imagination — all because my spelling was so bad!

"However, one night I was flicking through the channels on the TV when this program caught my eye. It was about this boy who really struggled with reading and writing at school, until he was diagnosed with something called dyslexia. He'd then gone on to excel at maths and had even won a place at university!

> "I always cringed when we had a spelling test."

"I could feel my heart thumping in my chest while I watched — it sounded just like me! I ran through to my mum and told her to switch it on — after a while she agreed that I might have it. It sounds weird but I remember going to bed feeling a lot happier than I had in ages that night…

"We went to the doctors the following week and, after a few tests, I was diagnosed with dyslexia! It's hard to explain — it's not that I wanted to have it, but it was just such a relief to find out that I wasn't just thick and that what I had was actually a recognised condition!

"I also found out that people with dyslexia are often talented in other areas, like art and music. That's why there are loads of celebrities with it, I guess. It also explained why I was good at creative writing but useless at other stuff like spelling.

"My parents took me up to the school for a meeting with my year head. The teachers have now been made aware of the fact that I have dyslexia and are a lot more understanding — and I've even been provided with a laptop in English so that I can use the spell check function to help me!

> "The teachers are a lot more understanding."

"I won't pretend that school isn't still tough for me sometimes, but for now I'm just glad the teachers can finally see that I'm not just lazy! I'm just so glad I saw the TV show — it's completely changed my life!"

> ▮ If dyslexia is becoming a problem for you then please log on to www.bdadyslexia.org.uk or try talking things over with a trusted parent, guardian or teacher.

what's your colour match?

Discover the ideal shade for you!

start

Your mates call you the funny one
— yes
— no

Winter is your fave season!
— yes
— no

Keeping secrets is easy!
— no
— yes

You love going to the cinema
— no
— yes

You're always texting
— no
— yes

Boys make great mates
— yes
— no

Scarves are super stylish!
— no
— yes

Are you always looking in the mirror?
— no
— yes

Hate being the centre of attention?
— yes
— no

You follow the latest trends
— no
— yes

Dark Colours
You totally suit dark colours! If you want to look your best, we think you should rock out in something dark. Black goes with everything!

Bright 'N' Bold
Grab everyone's attention in something brilliantly bright! You'll turn heads wherever you go. Neon pink would look amazing on you!

Perfect Pastel
You're super girlie and would look fab in neutral colours. A statement clutch would finish your outfit of perfectly!

49

WHAT LADS LOVE!

Now, these are the type of lads we like a lot!...

WE ASKED THESE BOYS WHAT THEIR FAVE THINGS ABOUT GIRLS IS...

"It's all about the eyes... that bit of magic when you make eye contact across a busy room. You can't beat that!"
Reece, 14

"I love a girl who knows who she is, what she wants and how to get it!"
Craig, 14

"Sure, I love gorgeous girls — but personality is definitely the most important thing."
Martin, 15

"I'm a total sucker for cute hair accessories like bows."
Kurt, 14

"I like how they think differently about most things. Who wants someone to just agree with you all the time? Not me!"
Eddie, 15

"I love everything about girls — I can't get enough of 'em!"
Lee, 15

"A good sense of humour goes a long way with me."
Liam, 16

"I used to pretend that it annoyed me, but I like it when my girlfriend borrows my clothes."
Kris, 15

"I like stunning-looking girls, ha ha!"
Darren, 16

"I like how girls don't play games and are honest with their feelings."
Ashley, 16

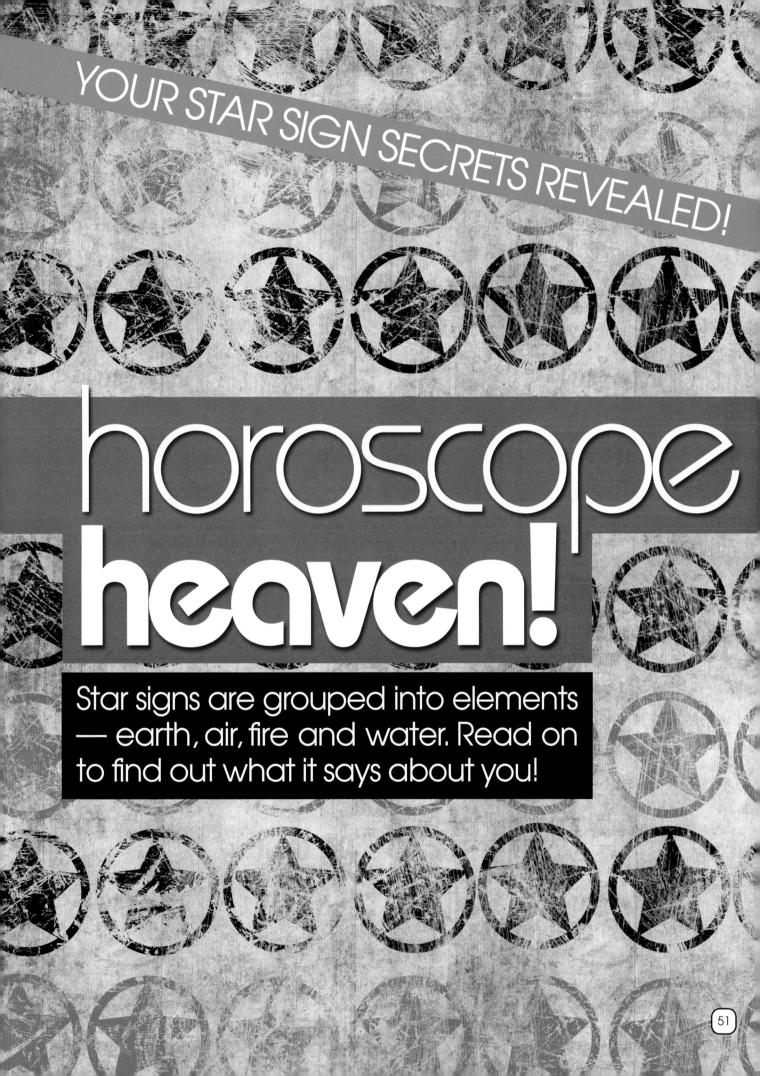

horoscope heaven!

Star signs are grouped into elements — earth, air, fire and water. Read on to find out what it says about you!

fire

**Aries
Leo
Sagittarius**

You live life to the full and get excited about, oh, everything! You're warm-hearted and friendly with almost everyone you meet so you're never short of mates. People can't resist being your friend cos you make them feel happy and encourage them to try new things... even if they don't want to!

ARIES
March 21 – April 20

Kristen Stewart
April 9, 1990

You're never scared of change and love taking charge of a situation (you secretly love being bossy!). If anyone's in a crisis, you know exactly what to do and you're fast on the track to fixing their problems.

You crave excitement, but if something's boring, you'll move on without thinking twice. That's the beauty of your sign — you stick around long enough to be noticed but, in a flash, you're gone!

GOOD TRAITS:	BAD TRAITS:
ENERGETIC	IMPATIENT
AMBITIOUS	QUICK-TEMPERED
ENTHUSIASTIC	SELFISH
CONFIDENT	

★ AS A MATE... When mates are having a down day, they can count on you to make them smile again!

Get loved-up with...
Sagittarius, Leo, Aquarius.
No flirtin' with...
Taurus, Libra, Pisces.

LEO
July 24 – August 23

Demi Lovato
August 20, 1992

Hello, Little Miss Diva! Yes, that's you! All eyes have got to be on you at all times (because you're so fabulous) and you can have quite the temper tantrum if you're not the centre of attention.

That said, you're an enthusiastic and extremely loyal friend — sometimes people wish they had as much charisma as you!

GOOD TRAITS:	BAD TRAITS:
GENEROUS	BOSSY
WARM-HEARTED	INTERFERING
SPONTANEOUS	BOASTFUL
GENUINE	

★ AS A MATE... You're totally handy with fashion and beauty tips!

Get loved up with...
Aries, Sagittarius, Gemini.
No flirtin' with...
Aquarius, Capricorn, Virgo.

SAGITTARIUS
November 23 – December 22

Taylor Swift
December 13, 1989

We wouldn't be surprised if you're in the middle of planning some new adventure! Luckily, Sagittarian lasses are naturally athletic which means you've got plenty of energy to do all the crazy things you want to!

Personality-wise, you think honesty is the best policy and you're not shy about telling people exactly what you think. You don't mean to offend people — it's just how you express yourself!

GOOD TRAITS:	BAD TRAITS:
OPTIMISTIC	CARELESS
HONEST	TACTLESS
INTELLECTUAL	IRRESPONSIBLE
GOOD-HUMOURED	

★ AS A MATE... Movies, music, lads... You're the girl in the know! Your mates are never out of the loop with a bright lass like you!

Get loved up with...
Aries, Leo, Libra.
No flirtin' with...
Cancer, Scorpio, Capricorn.

earth

Taurus
Virgo
Capricorn

The phrase 'down-to-earth' was made for you! You don't shy away from hard work and you're very grounded which means no-one messes you about! And let's not forget that stubborn streak of yours! You probably find that you're the one organising parties and sleepovers — without you your mates would fall apart!

TAURUS
April 21 – May 21

Megan Fox
May 16, 1986

You're *sooo* determined and you'll stop at nothing until you've seen your plans right through to the end! That English assignment? Yep, you've probably been working on that for hours! This makes you a great mate too, though. You always help solve your friend's problems and you don't back down until they're happy again.

You feel secure when you've got lots of belongings, which can make you a bit of a shopaholic! New Look, anyone?

GOOD TRAITS:	BAD TRAITS:
PATIENT	JEALOUS
RELIABLE	GREEDY
LOVING	STUBBORN
DETERMINED	

★ AS A MATE... **Ooh, we bet your friends love to borrow stuff from your wardrobe!**

Get love up with...
Virgo, Capricorn, Cancer.
No flirtin' with...
Aries, Libra, Aquarius.

VIRGO
August 24 – September 23

Beyoncé
September 4, 1981

Miss Virgo's are always striving for perfection. And you're instantly recognisable too — we bet you've not got a hair out of place, have spotless make-up and crease-free clothes!

You're always trying to make things better and you're there in people's time of need. You're the band-aid of the zodiac! You never grudge spending time cheering up friends and family and you're a very special friend to have!

GOOD TRAITS:	BAD TRAITS:
MODEST	FUSSY
RELIABLE	WORRIER
ORGANISED	PERFECTIONIST
SENSIBLE	

★ AS A MATE... **Whenever your mates are in a sticky situation, you manage to get 'em out of it.**

Get loved up with...
Taurus, Capricorn, Scorpio.
No flirtin' with...
Gemini, Leo, Pisces.

CAPRICORN
December 23 – January 20

Frankie Sandford
January 14, 1989

You're ambitious and want to succeed in everything you do. Others might think you can be too serious at times, but you'll have the last laugh when your hard work pays off and you're rich and famous!

But, even though you're poker faced about things like homework, you've actually got an amazing sense of humour and can make absolutely anyone laugh!

GOOD TRAITS:	BAD TRAITS:
INDEPENDENT	CONTROL-FREAK
WITTY	SERIOUS
PRACTICAL	CAUTIOUS
AMBITIOUS	

★ AS A MATE... **Hard-working and organised — your friends would be lost without you!**

Get loved up with...
Taurus, Virgo, Pisces.
No flirtin' with...
Gemini, Leo, Sagittarius.

air

Gemini
Libra
Aquarius

All the air signs are super intelligent, talkative and have amazing new ideas! You can see things from a different perspective which makes you a great problem solver. At a party, you'll be the one mingling and chatting to everyone and being totally fabulous! And of course, you love keeping up with the latest trends!

GEMINI
May 22 – June 21

Molly King
June 4, 1987

Gemini's symbolised by twins — which would explain your crazy personality! Your mates struggle to keep up with you and your moods — one minute you're the life and soul of the party, the next you're sulking cos your crush won't ask you out — but that's why they love ya!

You're a hoot to be around and your conversation's always hilarious. Just beware you don't over-indulge!

GOOD TRAITS:	BAD TRAITS:
TALKATIVE	NERVOUS
LIVELY	SUPERFICIAL
HAPPY	SHALLOW
THOUGHTFUL	

★ AS A MATE... You're their juicy goss/celeb news/rumour bible!

Get loved up with…
Aquarius, Libra, Leo.
No flirtin' with…
Cancer, Virgo, Capricorn.

LIBRA
September 24 – October 23

Nicola Roberts
October 5, 1985

Hey there, Miss Popular! You're so fun-loving and sociable that everyone wants to have you at their party! And boy, do you know how to party in style!

But you've got a sweet side too — you're ace at lending a sympathetic ear to friends in trouble. You've got the whole package!

GOOD TRAITS:	BAD TRAITS:
CHARMING	INDECISIVE
EASY-GOING	VAIN
FLIRTY	CARELESS
GENTLE	

★ AS A MATE... Your pals are lucky to have a party planner like you — there's never a dull moment!

Get loved up with…
Aquarius, Gemini, Sagittarius.
No flirtin' with…
Taurus, Scorpio, Pisces.

AQUARIUS
January 21 – February 19

Holly Willoughby
February 10, 1981

Ooh, you're such a mate magnet! You're so friendly and charming that no-one can resist being around you! It helps that you're a total gossip queen who's always got the latest juicy news!

You're never in the same place for long and you've always got an exciting plan up your sleeve. Life's never dull with you around!

GOOD TRAITS:	BAD TRAITS:
FRIENDLY	UNPREDICTABLE
ORIGINAL	UNEMOTIONAL
INDEPENDENT	DIFFICULT
HONEST	

★ AS A MATE... As long as you're at a party or a sleepover, it's guaranteed to be a fun night!

Get loved up with…
Gemini, Libra, Aries.
No flirtin' with…
Cancer, Scorpio, Taurus.

water

Cancer
Scorpio
Pisces

Everyone needs a water sign in their life — they understand how people feel, help with problems and will put their own problems on the line to help out a mate. You can even be a little bit psychic at times! You like dreaming, so it makes you especially good at art and music!

CANCER
June 22 – July 23

Cheryl Cole
June 30, 1983

No-one really knows the real you — on the outside you're a tough cookie but underneath you're really just a big softie.

Your mood changes from one minute to the next — you can go from moody to a ray of sunshine in 0–60 seconds! But whatever your mood, you're generous to a fault and will do anything for your mates.

GOOD TRAITS:	BAD TRAITS:
PROTECTIVE	MOODY
LOVING	OVER-EMOTIONAL
IMAGINATIVE	UNTIDY
PROTECTIVE	

★ AS A MATE... You put their needs before yours but if they're a good friend, they'll return the favour!

Get loved up with…
Scorpio, Pisces, Taurus.
No flirtin' with…
Gemini, Sagittarius, Aquarius.

SCORPIO
October 24 – November 22

Katy Perry
October 25, 1984

You don't let anyone mess around with the people you care about! You take a stand against bullies and won't put up with anyone's nasty behaviour. You're fiercely loyal to your friends and family.

But you're not all doom and gloom — you actually relate really well to others and your mates feel safe telling you their deepest, darkest secrets. You're the one who laughs and cries the hardest!

GOOD TRAITS:	BAD TRAITS:
PASSIONATE	JEALOUS
EXCITING	SECRETIVE
MYSTERIOUS	AGGRESSIVE
EMOTIONAL	

★ AS A MATE... You stick up for your mates and won't let anyone take advantage of them!

Get loved up with…
Cancer, Virgo, Pisces.
No flirtin' with…
Libra, Sagittarius, Aquarius.

PISCES
February 20 – March 20

Rihanna
February 20, 1988

Hello? Miss Pisces? You big daydreamer, you! You're Little Miss Talented and can turn your hand to writing, art and music.

You don't have a clue what you're doing from one day to the next which can be infuriating for everyone else around you, but it suits you just fine! You totally spark other people's imaginations and help them with creative tasks.

GOOD TRAITS:	BAD TRAITS:
SENSITIVE	SECRETIVE
COMPASSIONATE	DISORGANISED
KIND	IMPRESSIONABLE
SYMPATHETIC	

★ AS A MATE... Everyone wants a Pisces girl as their pal! Awww!

Get loved up with…
Cancer, Scorpio, Capricorn.
No flirtin' with…
Aries, Virgo, Libra.

"My Horoscope Came True!"

Kim found love — just like the stars said she would…

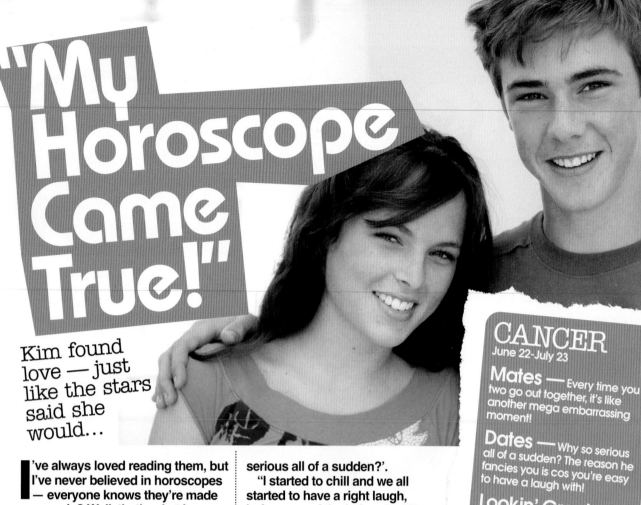

I've always loved reading them, but I've never believed in horoscopes — everyone knows they're made up, surely? Well, that's what I thought… until my *Shout* horoscope actually did come true!

"It all happened about six months ago and, although it didn't start off so well, it ended up being the best day of my life!

"I was going bowling with my best friend, Nadine, and it started to pour down with rain. We both only had skirts and skimpy tops on and got completely soaked.

"Worse was to come, though… as the first person we spotted was my crush and all his mates — typical! They were rolling about with laughter because we looked a right state. It was as if my horoscope was coming true, as it said that, 'Everytime you two go out together, it's like another mega embarrassing moment!'. Well, it definitely got that spot on!

"Things went from bad to worse for me when we decided we'd brave it and go over and talk to the guys. I was having a go at Leon for laughing at me when he told me to lighten up, as he wasn't being serious. What did my *Shout* horoscope say? It said, 'Why so serious all of a sudden?'.

"I started to chill and we all started to have a right laugh, before one of the lads asked if we wanted to share a bowling lane with them — result! I was praying that I'd get a chance to flirt with Leon when, suddenly, disaster struck…

> "I was praying that I'd get a chance to flirt with Leon."

"We were all queuing for drinks when a man accidentally bumped into me — spilling a whole cup of Coke right down my skirt.

"I knew straight away that I'd have to go home, as there was no way I could spend the afternoon covered in sticky cola… it was bad enough that I was still drenched from the rain — never mind this!

"As upset as I was about missing my big chance to score with Leon, there was nothing I could do other than laugh about it — everyone else was in stitches anyway! Nadine couldn't keep a straight face, but at least she offered to come home with me.

"Just before we left, however, Leon took me completely by surprise when he said he felt pretty bad about what had happened to me. He said that he'd always liked

> "It ended up being the best day of my life."

me as I was always up for a laugh — and then he asked me out!

"I was totally shocked, especially when I got home and started to read *Shout* again. It said, 'The reason he fancies you is cos you're easy to have a laugh with!' — almost exactly what Leon said to me. Now, surely this can't all have been a coincidence?!

"We had our first date at the bowling — it seemed appropriate! My horoscope said that my trend alert for that fortnight was denim shorts, so that's exactly what I wore — I wasn't leaving anything to chance! And, sure enough, Leon said that he thought I looked great!

"We're still seeing each other six months later — and *Shout* knew it was going to happen all along! So, the next time you read *Starspot*, don't be too surprised if it really does come true!"

WHAT'S YOUR secret obsession?

FASHION, FLIRTING OR SCANDAL? WHAT DO YOU LOVE?

start

Keeping a secret is hard!

yes / **no**

Celeb interviews are cool!

yes / **no**

The Saturdays are style queens

no / **yes**

Your bedroom wall is covered in posters of fit lads

yes / **no**

Gossip websites are your fave!

no

You believe every rumour you hear

yes / **no**

You keep up with all the latest trends

no / **yes**

You'd rather boy watch than shop!

no / **yes**

Pocket money is for saving!

yes / **no**

Mates always want to raid your wardrobe

yes / **no**

yes

BOYS

Hot boys like JLS are your weakness! You don't mind going to watch football when the lads on the team are all so fit. A flirty text puts you in a great mood, so get your mobile out and get texting...

GOSSIP

The latest celebrity scandal is the thing that makes you buzz! You're addicted to finding out what your fave celebs have been up to — whether it's good or bad!

FASHION

You're totally fashion fabulous! You'd rather be shopping and trying on clothes than gossiping with mates. There's no better feeling in the world than putting on that new dress!

57

A Best Mate Always...

THIS IS WHY YOU'RE BFFS...

■ Lets you borrow her fave outfit so you can impress your crush at the hot party — even though she was planning to wear it!

■ **Deletes any awful pics of you — they're, like, *sooo* not going on Facebook!**

■ Never lets boys come between you — so what if you both fancy the same hottie?!

■ Tells you when an outfit looks terrible — there's no way she'd let you go out looking like that!

■ Insists that there's no way your ex is over you — even though he's dating someone else and hasn't even looked at you since Splitsville!

■ Never forgets your birthday and doesn't give you grief when you (shamefully!) forget hers!

■ Lends you her deodorant after your dance class — well, she is gonna have to sit next to you on the bus home!

■ **Insists that the time you walked into class with toilet roll sticking out from your skirt wasn't actually that embarrassing — even though it totally was!**

■ Doesn't give the game away when you agree with your crush that the new Kings Of Leon song is great — even though she knows you can't stand them!

■ Lets you copy her homework that she spent, like, two hours on!

■ **Doesn't mind making convo with your crush's boring mate, so you can flirt away to your heart's content!**

10 superstar hotties!

*BEWARE! FAINTING MAY OCCUR ON THE FOLLOWING PAGES!

10

Joe Jonas

● We don't like having favourites, especially when it comes to the Jonas Brothers, but if we had to, HAD TO choose one, it would be Joe. Sorry, Nick and Kevin!

9

Dougie Poynter

● It's tough, but we picked one McFly boy and we've gone with the one that can make us laugh. Dougie's super talented too!

8

Chace Crawford

● *Gossip Girl's* mega babe Chace is pretty easy on the eye! So, we've decided to share the love with you! It's a hard job, but someone's got to do it!

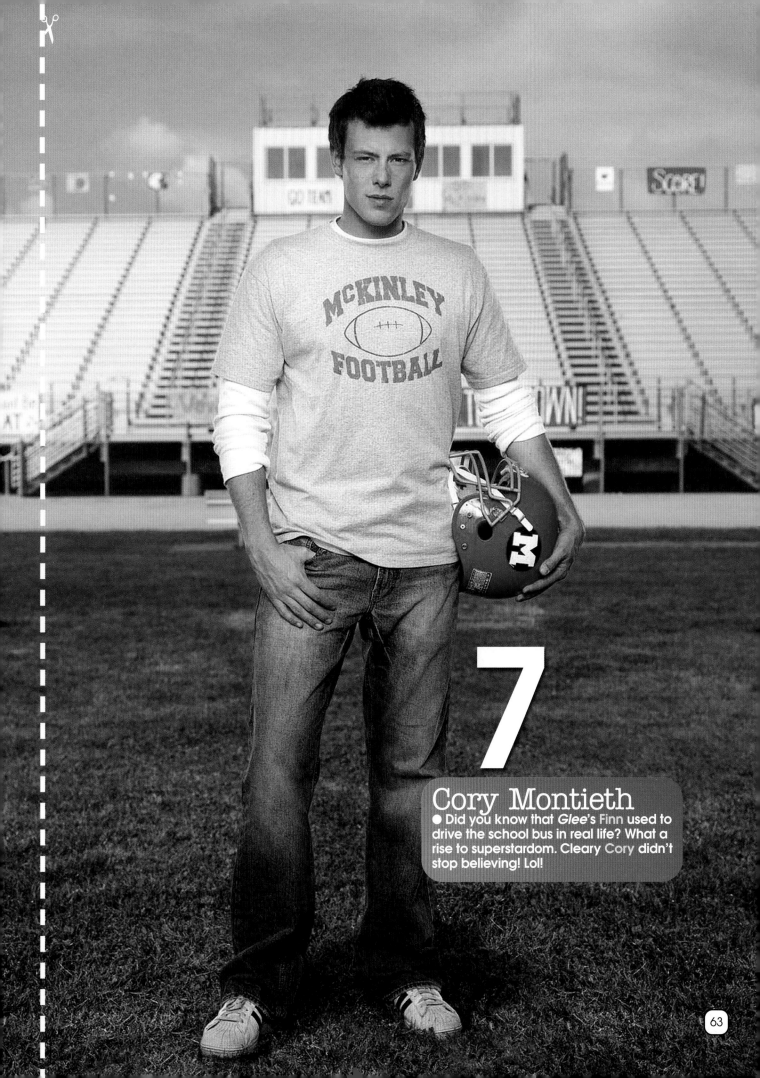

7

Cory Montieth

● Did you know that *Glee*'s Finn used to drive the school bus in real life? What a rise to superstardom. Cleary Cory didn't stop believing! Lol!

6
Channing Tatum
● He's hot, he's talented… he met his wife on the set of *Step Up*. Our hearts just broke into a million pieces…

5

Justin Bieber
● If you haven't experienced Bieber Fever yet, then surely it's going to hit you at some point. Symptoms include a racing heart, butterflies in your stomach and lack of concentration…

4

Taylor Lautner

● OK, whether you're Team Jacob or Edward, they're both FIT! Taylor has the most amazing smile and you've gotta respect a guy who put on 30lbs to keep his part in the *Twilight* films. What a star!

3

JLS
● We love the JLS boys so much that we couldn't possibly single one out. They're all so gorgeous and shout likes a boy that can sing!

2

Robert Pattinson

● Well, it looks like Team Edward has edged it! Anyone who doesn't think R-Pattz is lovely in every way needs their eyes tested. We're so jealous of Kristen Stewart! Grrrr.

1

Zac Efron

● Here he is, girls — **shout**'s No.1 hunk!
Mr Efron has proved himself to be HOT
when he acts, sings, dances and he's
super sweet in real life too. He's perfect
in every way. Congratulations, Zac!

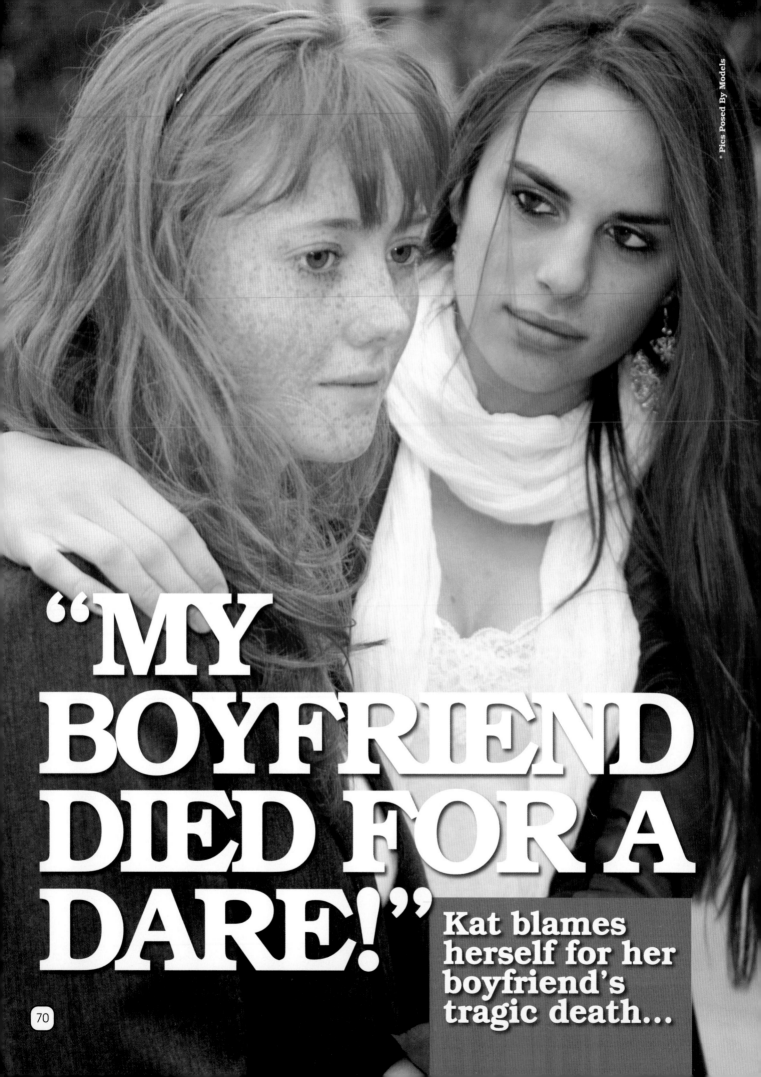

"MY BOYFRIEND DIED FOR A DARE!"

Kat blames herself for her boyfriend's tragic death...

I fancied Danny as soon as he moved to our area, and I was so happy when he asked me out. However, now I wish that I'd never even met him. You're probably wondering why, right? Well, it's because if I hadn't met him then he'd probably still be alive…

"There isn't much to do where I live, and one day one of the lads in our group suggested hanging about in this abandoned warehouse close by. Someone had ripped the boards off the windows and the floors were great for skateboarding.

"It was me that suggested we started playing truth or dare. I don't know why really — I guess I was hoping someone would dare me and Danny to kiss or something! The first few dares were pretty tame — like downing a can of coke without laughing — so it wasn't long till we were looking for something more exciting…

"It was then that one of the lads pointed at this high beam near the ceiling. I felt dizzy even looking at it but before I knew what was happening, Danny was getting dared to walk along it.

"He was the only one of us that hadn't done a dare so far and all the lads started egging him on, calling him a chicken and making clucking noises. I hate to admit now, but I even joined in. I knew he'd never hear the end of it if he refused…

"My heart was still in my mouth when he started climbing this rusty old ladder on the wall, though. Everyone started chanting his name as he made his way up and gave him a round of applause as he pulled himself up next to the beam. It all seemed like a big joke…

"I was really nervous when Danny took his first couple of steps onto the beam — but he just started playing up to his audience, flailing his arms around and acting like he was about to fall! Everyone was laughing but I couldn't help thinking that he was really high up…

"Then, a few steps later, Danny started waving his arms about again. I thought for a moment that he was joking around again, but then I realised that he'd lost his balance — for real this time. For a few horrible seconds we all just stood staring at him, completely helpless, before he started to fall…

"He let out this horrible scream, before landing on his back on the concrete floor. We all stood frozen for a second, before running over. Blood was coming out of his nose and Danny wasn't moving and I just didn't know what to do. I was screaming his name over and over but he didn't answer…

"Someone phoned for an ambulance and I remember thinking that it would all be OK once they got here. I was too scared to touch him in case I hurt him even more, but they'd know what to do to make him better, right?

"The ambulance came to take him away and the police took us home. They asked us loads of questions but I could barely even look them in the eye. I felt so guilty sitting there and telling them that all this had happened because of a stupid dare! I just wanted to know that Danny was OK…

"However, eventually a police woman took me to the side and quietly explained that Danny had died on the way to the hospital. He'd suffered massive injuries from the fall and there was nothing that anyone could do. I thought I was going to be sick! One minute we were having a laugh… now my boyfriend was dead.

"The next few days were a total blur. There was a special assembly at school in memory Danny but I just couldn't stop crying. It was even worse when a police officer spoke to the whole school about the dangers of trespassing abandoned in buildings. I felt like everyone was whispering about me and blaming me for his death…

"And that's exactly what Danny's parents thought — they refused to let any of us who were there that day to attend the funeral. They thought we'd egged him on and if it wasn't for us, he'd still be here. The worst part is that it's all true — we did. I just wish they knew how sorry I am…"

> "Everyone was laughing but I couldn't help thinking that he was really high."

> "I felt like everyone was whispering about me and blaming me for his death."

embarrassing moments!

Check out these crazy cringes!

Illustration by Michelle Draycott

RED-FACED RATING: 😊😊😊

■ "I was meeting my crush for a date and was really nervous, so I decided to give myself a bit of a makeover for some date confidence. I was wearing this gorge new dress and decided to dye my hair red so I would look totally hot… Big mistake! The hair dye worked great and my hair was looking perfect, but when I dried my hair and looked in the mirror I was shocked — the dye had stained my face! I looked absolutely ridiculous and had to cancel the date! Plus everyone teased me at school the next day! Eek!"
HAYLEY, EDINBURGH

RED-FACED RATINGS:

GET OVER IT! **SLIGHTLY SHAMEFUL!** **COMPLETELY CRINGEY!**

■ "I was shopping with my mates when I saw my crush over in the guys section, so I decided to creep up behind him to give him a fright! I sneaked up behind him and jumped on his back and shouted 'Boo!' and he screamed so loud and threw me off his back! I fell and knocked over this massive rail of clothes and they went everywhere! Everyone was staring at us and my mates were laughing so much… but when I looked up to see where my crush was I realised that it wasn't him, but some random guy! Oops!"

BETH, WARWICKSHIRE

RED-FACED RATING: 😀😀

■ "I was out shopping with my bezzie when I tried out her new Heelys skate shoes. It was really fun skating around on them, but then I spotted my crush, so I tried to catch his attention. I was casually skating along past the food court, checking him out, when my mate suddenly screamed 'Look out!', but it was too late… I crashed into this table full of food and knocked it over! I was covered in food and the people sitting down were so angry at me! AND my crush and his mates were laughing at me as I ran out of there!"

SHELLEY, LONDON

RED-FACED RATING: 😀😀😀

■ "I was out clothes shopping with my mates to get some hot outfits for a party, when one of my mates lifted up this massive minging top and asked me if I liked it. It was so gross, so I shouted back 'Ewww, it's so horrible, it's hurting my eyes!' when my friend just started laughing… She had tricked me — there was a woman standing right behind me, wearing the exact same top! She gave me the biggest dirty look ever as she walked past, while all my mates were in hysterics at me! So cringey!"

LOUISE, CARDIFF

RED-FACED RATING: 😀

CHECK OUT THIS BOY CRINGE!

■ "I was swimming with my mates when we spotted some girls from my class. I decided to impress them by doing a cool dive off the top diving board. I climbed up the ladder, ran and leaped off, trying to do a backflip before I landed in the pool — big mistake! I did the most painful belly flop ever, and I lost my trunks in the water! Then, my mates got my trunks and ran off with them! All the girls were laughing at me and I had to get a lifeguard to get me a towel to cover up! I'm still cringing now!"

JAY, LIVERPOOL

RED-FACED RATING: 😀😀😀

■ "I was at my school disco and was having the best time with my mates! I was wearing this glam new dress and was even getting cosy with my crush all night — the whole night was going perfectly! Then later on in the night, the DJ had a competition to see who was the hottest dancer… and I won! I was so happy that I rushed onstage to get my prize, but I slipped in my heels and fell in front of everyone with my knickers on show! The whole school was laughing at me including my crush! It was the worst day ever!"

CHLOE, ABERDEEN

RED-FACED RATING: 😀😀😀

■ "I was hanging out with my crush and my mates and I was quite confident that my flirting was going well. I could totally tell that he was flirting back and he was telling these really funny jokes. It was great until he told this hilarious joke… and I laughed so much that a massive bogey bubble came out of my nose! He was laughing so much at me, and all of my mates were laughing and teasing me too! It was so cringey, and everyone still annoys me about it! I don't think my crush will ever fancy me now! Eek!"

GILLIAN, LONDON

RED-FACED RATING: 😀😀😀

73

10 tips to make you a great mate!

Guarantee best friend status with these top tips!

1. Write!
A note, a cute card or even just a mini post-it... keep in touch the old-fashioned way and she'll know you mean it when you say she's your best friend.

2. Be Original!
Think of different ideas for the weekend and fun things you can enjoy doing together! This winter, why not plan a themed slumber party, hit the ice rink for some boy-spotting, or just munch mince pies with a girlie movie?!

3. Listen!
Whether it's the lad she likes or the album she can't wait to download, pay attention so when it comes to birthdays or special occasions... present-buying will be a breeze!

4. Make Her Smile!
Bake her a cake (or buy cupcakes and ice them yourself), fill a photo album with silly snaps of you both, or just send her a fun picture message!

5. Text!
A random 'You look GREAT!' text (even if you're together at the time!) will mean the world to your mate and give her an instant buzz!

6. Keep A Secret!

It seems a bit obvious but it's one of the most important secrets to being a trusted pal! No gossiping, no bitching, no backstabbing… or you'll lose that amazing mate! Gossip about celebs instead!

7. Think!

Think about the things she likes and she'll feel special when you remember. A mix CD of the best party tunes, an e-mail with a discount voucher for her fave shop, a silly poster with her head stuck next to Zac's… It's the little things and thoughts that count — and they don't cost you anything!

8. Be Yourself!

Be honest, don't pretend to be something you're not and stand up for what you believe in. Three simple ways to earn trust and respect from your friends. When it comes to dodgy haircuts however, the odd white lie is perfectly acceptable!

9. Be A Cheerleader!

Yep — hers! Congratulate your friend on her successes and be (genuinely) happy when things go well! It'll give you a confidence boost too, knowing that you're making someone else feel good!

10. Share!

You know that perfume she's always banging on about… that's sitting in your bedroom? Well, go on and give her a lend! The same applies for your fave dress, your fake tan and your phone when she needs to text that hot lad!

what's your PERFECT PARTY?

DISCOVER HOW TO MAKE YOUR NIGHT AMAZING!

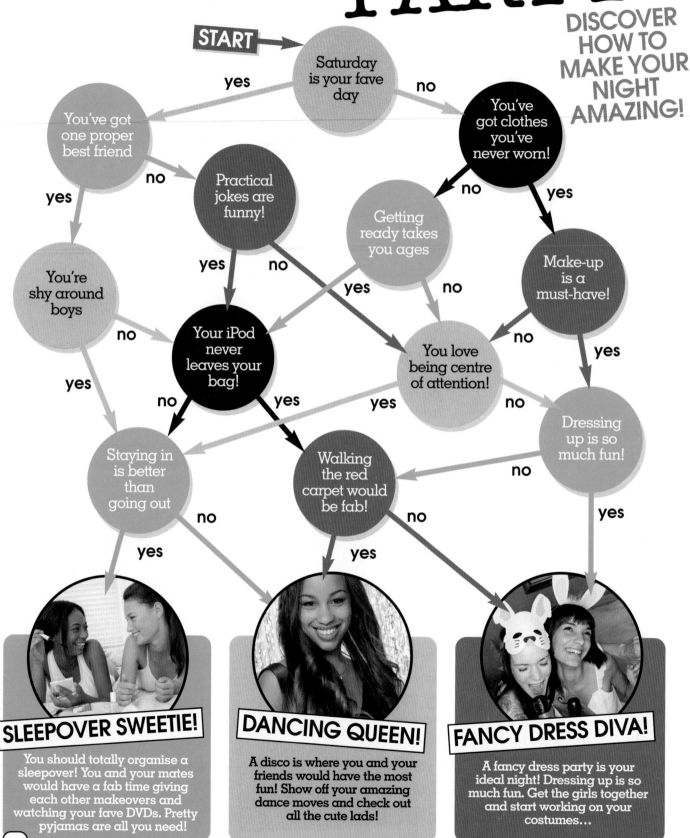

START → Saturday is your fave day

yes → You've got one proper best friend

no → You've got clothes you've never worn!

You've got one proper best friend: no → Practical jokes are funny!

You've got one proper best friend: yes → You're shy around boys

You've got clothes you've never worn!: no → Getting ready takes you ages

You've got clothes you've never worn!: yes → Make-up is a must-have!

Practical jokes are funny!: yes → Your iPod never leaves your bag!

Practical jokes are funny!: no →

Getting ready takes you ages: yes →

Getting ready takes you ages: no → You love being centre of attention!

You're shy around boys: no → Your iPod never leaves your bag!

You're shy around boys: yes →

Make-up is a must-have!: no → You love being centre of attention!

Make-up is a must-have!: yes → Dressing up is so much fun!

Your iPod never leaves your bag!: no → Staying in is better than going out

Your iPod never leaves your bag!: yes → Walking the red carpet would be fab!

You love being centre of attention!: yes →

You love being centre of attention!: no → Dressing up is so much fun!

Staying in is better than going out: no →

Staying in is better than going out: yes → SLEEPOVER SWEETIE!

Walking the red carpet would be fab!: yes → DANCING QUEEN!

Walking the red carpet would be fab!: no →

Dressing up is so much fun!: no → Walking the red carpet would be fab!

Dressing up is so much fun!: yes → FANCY DRESS DIVA!

SLEEPOVER SWEETIE!

You should totally organise a sleepover! You and your mates would have a fab time giving each other makeovers and watching your fave DVDs. Pretty pyjamas are all you need!

DANCING QUEEN!

A disco is where you and your friends would have the most fun! Show off your amazing dance moves and check out all the cute lads!

FANCY DRESS DIVA!

A fancy dress party is your ideal night! Dressing up is so much fun. Get the girls together and start working on your costumes…

H&M

Jane Norman

Miss Selfridge

George at Asda

Claire's

Matalan

faux fur
FABULOUS!
Fashionistas should go faux to keep the cold at bay!

HOW TO WEAR FAUX FUR:

▒ Dark indigo jeans tucked into boots and a faux fur jacket is a stunning day-time look! Or try it Diana-style with a flash of bright colour…!

▒ For the fashion fearful… Try ear muffs, a hat or bag!

▒ Make sure fake fur looks and feels soft — you don't want that dragged-through-a-hedge-backwards look!

▒ Leopard print styles call for a simple and elegant outfit — just say no to Pat Butcher earrings!

▒ A faux fur shrug is perfect party wear!

All products available at time of press.

Don't be caught out by the camera! Follow these top tips for taking photos!

picture *perfect!*

Tip 1
Act Natural!

★ **There's nothing worse than seeing a photo of someone with a forced smile. The number one rule to taking a good photo is to be yourself. Your natural pose will help your beauty shine through!**

Tip 2
Fashion Fail!

★ Just because something is in fashion, it doesn't mean you have to wear it. You've gotta feel comfortable in whatever your wearing. Your make-up bag will also come in handy for touching up your lip gloss before the camera comes out!

Tip 3
Perfect Pose!

★ **Wanna know why A-listers always look so good in their photos? There are five things top photographers recommend…**
- ■ Stand up straight — it'll make you look taller.
- ■ Turn your body to the side — it's a really flattering angle, y'know!
- ■ Bend the front leg slightly and point your front foot towards the camera.
- ■ Place one, or both hands on your hips.
- ■ And finally… SMILE!

Tip 4
Re-shoot!

★ Take a look at your photo once it's been taken. If your eyes are closed/hair's out of place, then get posing again! No-one will know how many photos you took to look fabulous!

Tip 5
Practise, practise, practise!

★ **Get in front of the mirror and perfect your amazing pose! When those photos turn up on Facebook everyone will wonder who that gorgeous girl is!**

Katy's perfected her pose!

5 GREAT FIRST DATES!

Follow **shout**'s top tips to hot date heaven!

Hot Date No.1 — Cinema
Perfect for shy girls!

■ **Why it's hot** — The cinema is a perfect date for girls who aren't mega confident about chatting away with that buff boy just yet. It lets you get up close and cosy without having to worry too much about what to say all the time! For a fun first date, go for a comedy or an action-packed blockbuster to keep that boy happy (save the rom-coms for when you've bagged that boyf)!

■ **Date Tip** — If you want to do the cinema without skimping on the chat, make sure you arrange plenty of talk time before or after the date!

Hot Date No.2 — Gig
Perfect for rock chicks!

■ **Why it's hot** — Rocking out at a gig with the lush lad that you're crushing on is always a great way to show him that you're confident, easy-going and that you've got loads in common with him, like loving the same music! Plus, when the date is over, you'll have loads of gig stuff to talk about!

■ **Hidden Date Drama** — Gigs can unfortunately get hot and can lead to frizzy hair, so be sure to carry a handy pocket sized Vaseline with you to act as an emergency all-in-one! A tiny dab can be a great frizz tamer, a cheek highlighter and a lovely lipbalm for extra kissable lips!

Hot Date No.3
— Home
Perfect for girls on a budge!

■ **Why it's hot** — This is THE best first date if you're totally date confident — all you have to do is show up and be yourself! What's not to love about it! This free date is ideal to scope out his room or for you to show off yours; and there are loads of things to do together, like playing Wii, watching a DVD or simply chatting away!

■ **Date Tip** — Make sure that if the date is at your place that you hide all your cringey crush stuff, and that there's no dirty laundry on show!

Hot Date No.4 — Bowling
Perfect for sporty girls!

■ **Why it's hot** — Bowling is a great casual date which lets you show off your fun personality as well getting to know him! You can get mega-flirty by asking him to help with bowling technique and you can totally check out your crush when it's his turn to bowl!

■ **Hidden Date Drama** — Bowling shoes! They don't go with any outfit, they never come in heels and they're so mingin'… They look like two different shoes that are sewn up the middle! Whoever designed them should be arrested for crimes against fashion!

Hot Date No.5
— Fast Food Joint
Perfect for chatty chicks!

■ **Why it's hot** — It's just you, him and some tasty treats — sounds like date heaven to us! A fast food date is great because it's relaxed, lets you talk away to each other away from friends and family and is THE perfect cheap and cheerful date! If talking to your crush doesn't freak you out too much then this date is the one for you!

■ **Date Tip** — Watch out for messy food! You don't want to end up with your fave dress covered in gherkins and ketchup, so make sure you keep your cool and order a mess-free meal like chicken nuggets and fries!

Friend or Frenemy?

Find out here!

Have you ever...

- [ ] Stolen your friend's fashion look?

- [ ] Blabbed her biggest secret?

- [ ] Read her diary?

- [ ] Borrowed stuff that you, erm, accidentally-on-purpose forgot to give back?

- [ ] Secretly copied her schoolwork?

- [ ] Put her off a lad... just so you could ask him out!

- [ ] Told her she looks great, when she really looked so, sooo bad?

- [ ] Started a rumour about her?

- [ ] Played a practical joke on her that was a bit mean?

- [ ] Let her take the blame for something that you did?

How many boxes did you tick?

1 – 3 Great Mate

You stick by your bezzies no matter what and always help them out when they're in a sticky situation! You'd never deliberately hurt a mate's feelings and always apologise straight away when you step out of line! If only everyone had friends like you!

4 – 6 Not Bad BFF!

Well... you're not so innocent when it comes to committing a friendship faux pas, but even good mates make mistakes. So put those pal problems in the past and be there for your mates from now on! Anyway, it's not as if those mate mishaps were that bad... were they?

7 – 10 Frenemy!

Ooh, shame on you! You're officially on the BFF blacklist — committing every friendship crime we can think of! Seriously though, you have to take better care of your mates if you want to keep 'em — before they trade you in for someone nicer! Oops!

are you
body confident?

Figure out what gives you the blues!

start

You ♥ a pampering sesh!
— no →
— yes ↓

You're a Gok Wan fan!
— no →
— yes ↓

Shopping is *sooo* boring
— no ↓
— yes ↓

You're comfortable in a bikini
— no →
— yes ↓

You know how to dress for your shape
— no →
— yes ↓

You're always on a diet
— no ↓
— yes ↓

You hate wearing shorts in P.E.
— yes ↓

You carry a compact mirror around with you
— no →
— yes ↓

You know how to pose!
— no →
— yes ↓

Changing rooms = nightmare!
— no ↓
— yes ↓

BODY BRILLIANT!

Wow! You're one confident chick! You love looking after yourself by exercising, eating healthily and having the odd pampering sesh! You know you're not 100% perfect — but who is?! You celebrate what you've got, girl!

BODY BLAH!

You don't hate what you see… But you don't heart it either! Some days you feel great about yourself and other days you just wanna stay in bed. You know how to dress for your shape though, so start focusing on the bits you do like and you'll soon love yourself!

BODY BLUE!

You can be totally harsh on yourself and other people don't know why. To them, you look fab! Sometimes you can obsess over something you don't like so much that it takes over your life. Follow **shout**'s fashion tips to find out how to dress for your shape and get your mate to give you a girlie makeover — sorted!

83

ENTRY

Sort out the cringe-o-rama with these top tips!

the EX factor

Dealing with... *HIS* Ex!

Problem 1: He talks about her...

■ If he can't get through a sentence without mentioning the-name-that-should-never-be-mentioned then, trust us, you're not overreacting! Try dropping your ex into the convo to see how he likes it (not much, we think!) or just having a quick chat with him. No big deal!

Problem 2: She wants him back!

■ Don'tcha just love it? You meet a cute lad, you think he's great, but you *soooo* hadn't bargained on him having a loopy ex-girlfriend who refuses to leave him alone! The best thing to do is to just not get involved — no bitching, no silly PDAs and no getting insecure. He's with you, so chill!

Dealing with... *YOUR* Ex!

Problem 1: Being just 'friends'...

■ Oh right, you're just being 'friendly' when you call/text/hang out with him every night, just like you did when you were all loved up. Pull the other one, missy! You don't get over a relationship in 24 hours (unless your name is Katie Price!) so it's best to take some time out from each other...

Problem 2: The new gf — eek!

■ We know how this one goes... you hate her if she's pretty/skinny/popular — and you hate her just as much if she's not! However, bleating about this fact will just make you look like the 'Big Jealous Ex', so the best advice is to just keep it zipped... and be nice as pie if you ever meet!

TOP TIP!
Stop Facebook stalking! Logging onto his page to check that he's as miserable as you are is a really bad idea. Repeat after us, a *really* bad idea...

TOP TIP!
Mooning around with a I've-just-been-dumped face is not going to help matters, so keep yourself busy, hang out with your mates, and you *will* feel better!

Avoid the break-up bloodbath!

Dark red (or orange)...

- You love to hit the town and show off with your gang of girl friends!
- You really don't like to be caught without your make-up on!
- You're always latest with the scandal — whether it's Pete and Katie or school snogs, you're the gossip girl!

Black (or navy blue)...

- So chic — that's you! You're always dressed to impress!
- You're a bit of a boy magnet, aren't you? What a fabulous flirt!
- You've got expensive taste and love posh clothes!

Baby pink (or pastel colours)...

- You love to shop — especially when you're with your best mates!
- Your look is classy and cool — you know how to dress well!
- You're always eyeing up celeb style — if only you had Vanessa's wardrobe... sigh!

WHAT'S YOUR Nail Polish Personality?

Find out what your fingertips say about your style!

Purple (or lilac)...

- You're the girl everyone wants to be mates with — lucky you!
- You're always a step ahead of the trends — ooh, so stylish!
- You have a huge group of friends and are never short of a party invite!

Neon turquoise (or any bright colours)...

- You're loud, proud and you don't care what other people think!
- You can't help speaking your mind... all the time!
- You have loads of energy and are always coming up with fun plans for your friends!

Silver (or metallic shades)...

- You love a little metallic sparkle to makeover your nails...
- You can sometimes be shy but you're 100% yourself around your BFFs!
- You're such a loyal friend! No secrets cross your lips and you'll never bitch about your buds!

Are you aiming for the A-LIST?

WOULD YOU BE A SUPER CELEB OR ARE YOU JUST FAME HUNGRY?

START

Celebs have it easy

Rihanna is your fave!

You'd love to see yourself in a magazine

You ♥ being the centre of attention!

Reality TV rules!

Being papped would be so cool!

Getting your own way is important

You love the thought of people talking about you

Your Facebook is full of pics of you pouting

Your mates always ask for style tips

ABSOLUTE A-LIST!
You belong next to the top celebs! You always look super glam and you're mega-talented. You'd always make loads of time for your fans, too!

B-LIST BABE!
If you were a celeb you'd be more famous for your attitude than anything else! Your loud mouth means that no-one would pay attention to all the good stuff you do!

D-LIST DIVA!
You're going to be famous — one way or another! Your friends call you a diva because you always get your own way. A career in reality TV or a life as a WAG is definitely your destiny…

LAUGH OUT LOUD LAWS!

O.M.G.! Could these real-life laws *be* any weirder?!

I'M INNOCENT, HONEST!

■ In Scotland, it's illegal to refuse to let a stranger use your toilet! How gross?!

■ It's against the law to climb trees in Canada!

■ **Thankfully, it's illegal to hang a, erm... bed out of a window in England!**

■ It is illegal for a pig to be called Napoleon by its owner in France!

■ In Greece, you can lose your driving licence if the police think that you are poorly dressed or need a bath! Is this the fashion police?

■ Flushing the toilet after 10pm is banned in Switzerland — Ewww!

■ In Alabama, it's against the law to drive a car wearing a blindfold! Like, who would do that?

■ In Georgia, it is illegal to tie a giraffe to a street lamp!

■ Cats and dogs are forbidden to fight each other in North Carolina!

■ **In Oregon, it is unlawful to box or fight with a kangaroo!**

■ It's illegal to make ugly faces at a dog in Oklahoma!

■ In Kentucky, it's the law that a person must take a bath once a year. What, only once?

THAT'S QUACKERS!

WHO ARE YOU CALLING UGLY?

■ **In Washington, it's against the law to ride an ugly horse!**

89

party perfect!

Glamour queens will ♥ these fabulous beauty looks!

Party Trick: Liquid Liner

Make-up pros love this look!

Remember to flick out the ends for old school glamour!

Avon Sleek Lines Eyeliner

N.Y.C Liquid Eyeliner

Miss Sporty Fabulous Sorbet Lipgloss

Party Trick: Pink Lipgloss

Every girl worth her weight in make-up will be slicking this on before a party!

Too Faced Mirror Mirror Gloss

Party Trick:
Smoky Eyes

Sweep your lids with dressed-up charcoal colours and add a twinkling of silver in the corners of your eyes.

Maybelline
Expert Wear
Duo

Mac
Eyeshadow

Party Trick:
Body Gems

They're a versatile beauty touch we can't resist!
The corners of your eyes will sparkle under the fairy lights or, you can wear 'em as nail art!

Elegant Touch
Dimensional
Nail & Body
Rhinestone Kit

Perfect Girl
Stick On Gems

91

Mememe Beautifully
You Eyeshadow
Duo No. 5

Party Trick:
Purple
Eyeshadow

**Purple lids are a
seriously cool beauty
look.**
Wear it sheer with a hint of
glitter or go for bold block
colour for serious impact!

17 Trio
Eyeshadows
in Purple
Heart

The Body
Shop Glitter
Eyeliner in
Silver

Party Trick:
Glitter Liner

Get sparkling eyes in no time
by adding a touch of glitter
liner. It's mega easy to apply
and adds a touch of fun to
your look!

Technic
Glitter
Eyeliner
in Silver

Party Trick: Lengthening Mascara

Bump up your blinking power with seriously lengthening mascara!

Thick black lashes scream glamour puss so that's why we apply two coats!

Mememe
Drama Queen
Ultimate Diva
Lashes

Bourjois
Volume
Glamour
Ultra Black
Mascara

N.Y.C Colour Wheel
Mosaic Face Powder
All Over Bronze Glow

Collection 2000
Complete
Bronzing Kit

Party Trick: Shimmery Bronzer

Ok, so your face looks perfect... But why not add some shimmer to your body? Dust over shoulders, arms and down your legs for that ultra glam touch!

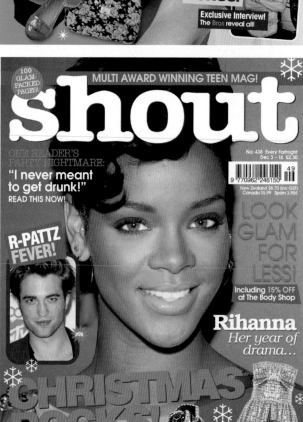